BATS

by Jennifer Zeiger

Children's Press®

An Imprint of Scholastic Inc.
New York   Toronto   London   Auckland   Sydney
Mexico City   New Delhi   Hong Kong
Danbury, Connecticut

Content Consultant
Dr. Stephen S. Ditchkoff
Professor of Wildlife Sciences
Auburn University
Auburn, Alabama

Photographs © 2013: age fotostock: 5 top, 19 (Gerard Lacz), 31
(R Koenig), 23 (WILLOCX Hugo); Bob Italiano: 44 foreground, 45
foreground; Dreamstime: 16 (Kison1979), 2 background, 3,
44 background, 45 background (Zzz777u); Getty Images/
Bob Stefko: 32; iStockphoto/Chris Slapp: 28; National
Geographic Stock/Joel Sartore: 4, 5 background, 40; Photo
Researchers/Dr. Merlin D. Tuttle/Bat Conservation International:
7, 20, 27; Photoshot: cover; Shutterstock, Inc./Ivan Kuzmin: 35;
Superstock, Inc.: 12 (age fotostock), 11 (Animals Animals), 1, 2
foreground, 8, 46 (Barry Mansell), 5 bottom, 24, 36 (Minden
Pictures), 15 (NHPA); USFWS Headquarters/Ryan von Linden/New
York Dept. of Environmental Conservation: 39.

Library of Congress Cataloging-in-Publication Data
Zeiger, Jennifer.
   Bats/by Jennifer Zeiger.
      p. cm.—(Nature's children)
   Includes bibliographical references and index.
   ISBN-13: 978-0-531-26830-8 (lib. bdg.)
   ISBN-13: 978-0-531-25475-2 (pbk.)
   1. Bats—Juvenile literature. I. Title.
   QL737.C5Z45 2013
   599.4—dc23   2012000634

1 2 3 4 5 6 7 8 9 10 R 22 21 20 19 18 17 16 15 14 13

Bats

Class	Mammalia
Order	Chiroptera; 2 suborders: Megachiroptera (Old World fruit bats) and Microchiroptera (small bats)
Families	1 Megachiroptera family; 17 Microchiroptera families
Genus	More than 200 genera
Species	More than 1,100 species
World distribution	Every continent except Antarctica, covering all regions except extreme arctic and desert areas
Habitats	Tropical, subtropical, and temperate forested areas
Distinctive physical characteristics	Hairless wings; fur-covered bodies; strong back claws; microbats have large ears; megabats generally have long, pointy faces
Habits	Almost all species are nocturnal; many use echolocation to hunt for prey; most live in groups
Diet	Fruit bats eat fruit, flowers, pollen, and nectar; other bats usually prefer insects, small mammals, frogs, fish, blood, or occasionally other bats

Contents

6 CHAPTER 1
Fascinating Flyers

10 CHAPTER 2
Creatures of the Night

21 CHAPTER 3
Bat Life

30 CHAPTER 4
Birds or Mice?

37 CHAPTER 5
Bats in Danger

42 Words to Know
44 Habitat Map
46 Find Out More
47 Index
48 About the Author

Fascinating Flyers

For centuries, people have been curious about bats. These strange animals fly like birds but are furry like mice. Their silent flight and nighttime hunts can make them seem mysterious. Bats' homes seem to come right out of a scary story. Many species like to hide in deep, dark caves and in the attics of old houses. Many people don't even know it when there are bats living in their homes. Other bats prefer to hang upside down like giant fruit from leafless trees. In some places, people consider bats a sign of bad things to come. People in other areas of the world think bats are good luck.

Bats have certainly made an impression on humans. But these animals are much more than myth. Their flight, hunting methods, and living arrangements are just a few of the things that make them unique.

Around sunset, bats leave their hiding places in caves and old buildings to search for insects in the night sky.

What Is a Bat?

Bats are one of the most **diverse** types of animal on Earth. There are more than 1,100 different species, ranging widely in size. The tiny bumblebee bat weighs just 0.07 ounces (2 grams), while the giant golden-crowned flying fox weighs around 3.3 pounds (1.5 kilograms). Some bats eat only fruit, while others eat insects, fish, or even blood.

However, all bats have a few things in common. Bats are the only **mammals** that can fly. Their wing **membranes** are their most recognizable features. They also move around by using the strong claws on their back feet and front thumbs to climb and cling to rocks and wood. Because they are mammals, all bats have fur. Most have very furry bodies with hairless wings. The fur on some bats, such as the hairless bat, can be harder to see.

Almost all bat species are **nocturnal**. This means they are awake at night and sleep through the day.

Adult Male
6 ft. (1.8 m)

Flying Fox
6 ft (1.8 m)

Kitti's hog-nosed bat
6 in (15.2 cm)

Bats have furry bodies and thin, mostly hairless wings.

CHAPTER 2

Creatures of the Night

Adult bats do not have many threats to worry about. Very few bats are killed by predators. However, there are a few animals that consider bats to be a tasty meal. Hawks and owls sometimes try to catch bats. Raccoons, snakes, house cats, and even other bats can pose a threat, too. These predators might sneak into bats' roosts while the bats are sleeping. They also sometimes attack baby bats that have fallen or been left alone by their parents.

Many of a bat's habits are designed to help keep it safe from predators. For example, most bats sleep in secluded, hard-to-reach areas. They rarely leave these hidden spots during the day, when many potential enemies are active. When they do leave their roosts, bats tend to stay high above the ground. This keeps them out of reach of most predators. Such behavior allows most bats to live long lives. Some species have been known to live for more than 20 years in the wild.

Though it is rare, bats are sometimes captured by predators such as snakes and birds.

Seeing with Sound

Bats hunt for **prey** at night. Many bat species use **echolocation** to help them make their way through darkened skies. Echolocation is the use of sound waves to "see" surrounding objects. A bat sends out high-pitched sounds either from its mouth or through its nose. When the sound waves hit an object, they bounce back, or echo. A person can get a similar result by yelling into a cave or down a well.

The bat listens for the echo with its large ears. Its brain notices how loud the echo is, how long it took to bounce back to the bat, and from which direction it came. This information tells the bat an object's size and shape, how fast it is moving, and in which direction it is traveling. The bat immediately knows whether the object is a tree, a rock, or its favorite species of moth.

FUN FACT! Sonar technology used by humans works much the same way as echolocation.

Bats use echolocation to avoid buildings and other obstacles.

13

Keeping an Eye Out

You may have heard the famous phrase "blind as a bat." However, bats actually have very good vision. Fruit bats have the best eyesight of all species. These bats live in the wet, warm rain forests of the tropics and subtropics. They don't use echolocation to find the fruits and flowers they eat. Instead, they depend on their eyesight and sharp sense of smell. Their eyes are very large, which allows them to take in as much light as they can. This makes it easier to see at night, when not much light is available.

Fruit bats use their sense of smell to help them track down the food they want to eat. They also smell the fruit to make sure it is ripe enough to eat. Species that eat pollen or nectar from flowers have long tongues. Small bristles on the tongue help the bat scoop out the nectar and pollen from deep inside the flower.

Flowers are a sweet treat for some bat species.

Flying the Distance

Bat species that live in temperate areas must work to avoid freezing when the weather turns cold. Many of these bats migrate. Each fall, they fly to places where the weather is warmer. They fly back home again in the spring. These trips can be very long. Mexican free-tailed bats travel up to 600 miles (965 kilometers) each fall as they fly from Texas and surrounding areas south to central Mexico. Some bats in North America and Russia fly even farther.

Fruit bats do not worry much about cold weather. Their tropical homes stay warm all year. However, fruit bats fly to where their favorite foods are growing. Those fruits ripen in different places at different times of year. The bats sometimes have to migrate to follow their food supply. For example, the gray-headed flying fox travels some 600 miles (965 km) across Australia to find the wild fruits and flowers that make up its diet.

Some fruit bats travel long distances to find food.

Sleeping Through Winter

Most bats protect themselves from the harsh winter weather by hibernating. Finding a place to hibernate sometimes requires a long trip, but most bats find winter roosts close to their summer homes. Long-eared bats often travel only a few miles.

Bats eat a lot of food before hibernating. A bat's weight increases around 25 to 30 percent on average during this time. This gives the bat energy to last through the winter. Saving energy is important. To do this, bats drop their body temperatures far below normal levels. A cold bat's heart rate goes down, which means the bat does not need to breathe as often. Bats move very little when hibernating. Some bats hibernate as long as six months. Other species enter a state similar to hibernation, called torpor. During the day, they enter a deep sleeplike state with lower body temperatures and heart rates. They wake up at dusk to hunt.

Hibernating bats often look as if they are simply sleeping.

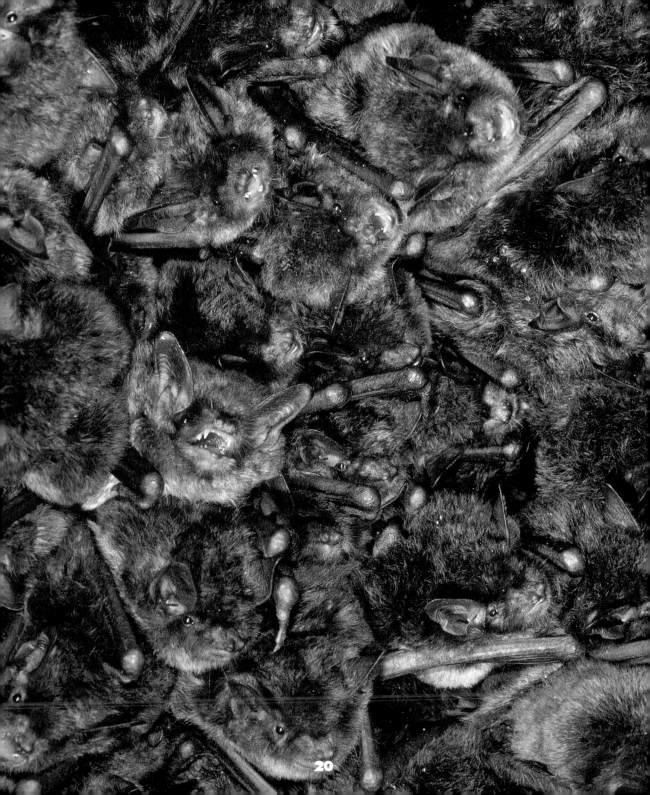

CHAPTER 3

Bat Life

Most bats live in colonies. Colonies can be enormous, with some made up of several million bats. Insects are the only animals to form larger groups. The largest bat colonies tend to form during winter, when several species often hibernate in the same place.

Not all bats live in giant colonies. Some bats spend the summer on their own or in groups of two or three. Some form pairs of one male and one female. Others form harems, which are made up of one male and a few females. Some smaller colonies are entirely female or entirely male.

Colonies are not usually permanent. Many bats, especially those in temperate areas, change their living arrangements throughout the year. For example, common pipistrelles spend their winters in mixed groups of thousands. In the summer, they live in colonies separated by gender and age. The bats move into harems as mating season begins in the fall.

Bat colonies often pack tightly together when roosting.

The Perfect Home

Bats choose their homes carefully. If a roost is too cold, a bat could freeze. If it is too hot, the bat could overheat. **Humidity** is also important. Dry air causes a bat's wings to lose moisture. Dry wings become brittle and tear easily.

Bats in warm areas often roost in plants. Flying foxes prefer to hang from tree branches. Smaller bats make homes out of palm or banana leaves. Three species of disk-winged bats even have special suction cups on their thumbs and feet to help them hold on to the leaves. In colder places, some bats sleep inside hollow trees.

Some bats live in caves. They cling to the rocky ceilings or hide underneath rubble on the floor. Old buildings can serve as substitutes for caves. Many bats roost in attics, basements, and any other places where they can find safe hiding spots.

Smaller bats can make their homes in the tiniest holes in trees.

What's for Dinner?

Most bats are insectivores. Insects form all or part of the diet for about 70 percent of bat species. A single bat can eat 3,000 mosquitoes in a single night. It might catch the insects in its mouth as it flies or scoop them up with its tail membrane if it has one.

After insects, the most common bat foods are fruits and flowers. These foods make up the diets of fruit bats and other tropical bats. Some bats eat fish, frogs, and other small animals.

Perhaps the most famous diet is that of the vampire bat. These incredible creatures feed on the blood of living animals. There are three species of true vampire bats. Most of them live in Central and South America, though one species is found as far north as northern Mexico. They usually feed on the blood of birds and cattle.

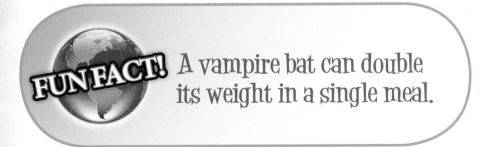

FUN FACT! A vampire bat can double its weight in a single meal.

Bats can swoop down to snatch insects from the surface of water or the ground, or grab them right out of the sky.

Baby Bats

Baby bats are helpless when they are first born. Most have little or no hair and are blind and deaf. Their wings are too small and weak for flying. Because of this, bat **pups** are completely dependent on their mothers. Bat mothers provide food, warmth, and safety until their pups are old enough to take care of themselves.

Most pups are born one at a time. Giving birth upside down can be risky. Most bat mothers avoid it by turning themselves sideways or right side up. While giving birth, the mother uses her tail membrane as a sort of net to catch the newborn pup. The pup clings to its mother with its strong back feet and front thumbs.

Less than half of all pups survive to become adults. Some starve to death. Others fall from their perches and cannot climb back up. Predators can also be a threat to the defenseless pups.

Bat pups have weak, hairless bodies.

Growing Up in an Upside-Down World

Pups spend most of their youth upside down clinging to their mothers. Like all mammals, bat mothers produce milk to feed their young. This means the pup always has easy access to food.

Bats that eat fruits and flowers take their young with them when finding food. Bat mothers that hunt insects and other animals cannot do this. The weight of the baby would make it difficult to chase down prey. These pups are left in the roost when their mothers go out to hunt. Often, a few females stay behind to watch over the colony's pups. After the hunt, the mothers find their young by following the pups' calls and scents.

Most pups begin flying when they are about a month old. They start to eat regular food soon afterward. Most bats are fully grown by the time they are a year or two old.

Bat pups begin to look more like their parents as they get older.

CHAPTER 4

Birds or Mice?

Bats have existed for a very long time. Scientists have found **fossils** from around 60 million years ago that might be related to bats. The fossils share some characteristics with bats, but scientists disagree about how closely related they are. Scientists agree that the oldest known bat fossil is about 45 million years old. Bats have not changed very much since that time. Their wings, diets, and basic body shape are mostly the same as they have been for millions of years.

In spite of these fossils, scientists are still asking questions about how to classify bats. People long ago argued over two basic theories. Because bats have wings and can fly, some believed that they were related to birds. But since they are also furry and have mouse-like faces, others believed them to be flying mice. Scientists today agree that neither theory was correct.

Fossils have taught scientists a great deal about the history of bats.

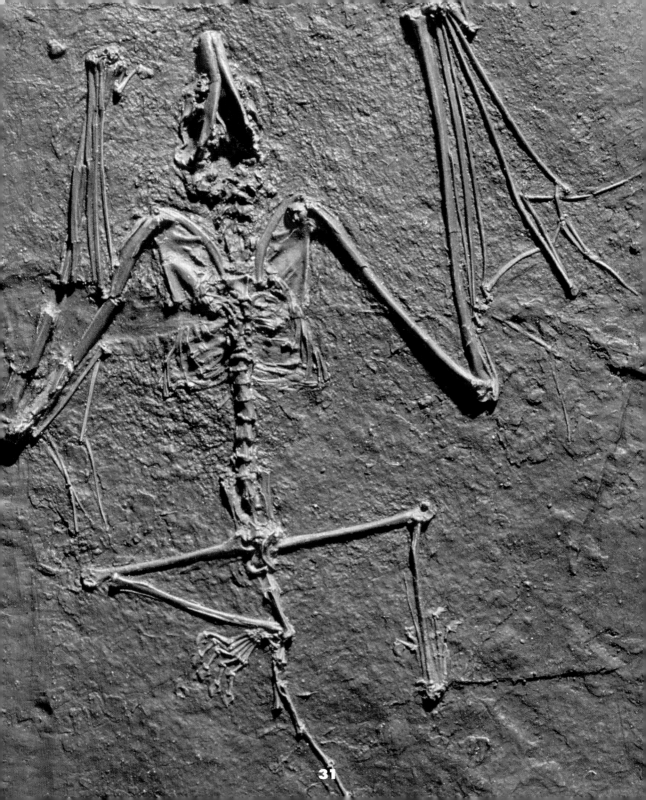

Mysterious Species

Scientists still do not know which animals are bats' closest relatives. Over the years, new studies and technology have given scientists a better understanding of bats. By the late 1800s, most scientists agreed that bats were neither birds nor mice. For much of the 20th century, scientists believed that bats were actually more closely related to humans and other primates. They argued that bats, especially fruit bats and flying foxes, have brains and physical features similar to monkeys and apes.

Another theory is that bats are more closely related to moles, musk shrews, and other insectivores. Some scientists have even connected them to camels, hippopotamuses, or whales. Many scientists simply argue that bats do not have any truly close relatives.

 **FUN FACT!** It is illegal to bring flying foxes into the United States without special permission.

Some bat species, such as flying foxes, have facial features similar to those of monkeys and other large mammals.

Megabats and Microbats

All bats belong to the order Chiroptera. This order is divided into two suborders called Megachiroptera, or megabats, and Microchiroptera, or microbats. Megabats are Old World fruit bats. *Mega* means "big," and Old World fruit bats are some of the largest bat species. Microbats make up the other bat families, including smaller fruit bats, insectivores, and other meat eaters.

Megabats and microbats are easy to tell apart. Megabats have long snouts and large eyes. Their ears are small compared to those of microbats. This is because most megabats do not use echolocation, so they do not have to listen for echoing sound waves. Microbats have flatter faces, smaller eyes, and very large ears for echolocation. Many microbats also have nose leaves. These are strangely shaped flaps of skin positioned over the nose. Scientists aren't sure what nose leaves are for, but many believe they help produce echolocation sounds.

Microbats often have very unusual-looking faces.

CHAPTER 5

Bats in Danger

Bats and humans have not always gotten along. In the past, bats were hunted either to make medicine or for superstitious reasons. These days, humans and bats often compete over the same habitats. Some bats, especially those that live in rain forests, are losing their homes to deforestation. Logging companies clear whole areas of forest. Elsewhere, bat habitats are destroyed to make room for new homes and farmland. Roosts are disturbed or destroyed.

Habitat loss forces bats into areas where humans live. They bother people by roosting in homes and other buildings. Many bats fly into farmland to feed on crops, which hurts farmers. Bats also carry diseases such as rabies. This is a problem especially with vampire bats. They can transfer these diseases when they bite cows or other prey. The illness can then pass among cows and cause major damage to a rancher's herd. As a result, ranchers hunt and kill vampire bats to protect their cattle.

Vampire bats can transmit deadly diseases to cattle and other prey.

White Nose Syndrome

Bats around the world suffer from parasites such as fleas, lice, and ticks. But bats in the eastern United States and Canada are making scientists nervous with a new sickness. The disease was first reported in early 2006, when a cave explorer found a group of hibernating bats whose noses had been turned white by a fungus. The cave was also filled with dead bats. Scientists studying the bats named the sickness white nose syndrome (WNS).

Bats suffering from WNS often hunt during the day or when other bats are hibernating. This means their preferred food is hard to find. They often sleep near the mouths of caves, where it is colder than the cave interiors. This behavior can cause them to starve or freeze.

Several more cases of WNS were reported in the following winters. The disease quickly spread. By 2010, WNS had killed more than one million bats as far west as Indiana and Kentucky.

White nose syndrome can quickly wipe out entire colonies of bats.

Protecting Bats

Scientists believe that WNS likely spreads when bat colonies encounter each other during migration. They are not sure how to stop it from spreading further. National and local governments encourage people to report any bats they notice behaving oddly. Organizations and government agencies use this information to keep track of where and how often WNS occurs.

Other bats also need help. In many places, it is illegal to harm or kill a bat, even if it has invaded a home, farm, or ranch. Some people build bat boxes, which are like birdhouses for bats. These can serve as alternate houses, to keep bats from roosting in people's homes. Bats living in these boxes help control nearby insect populations, providing an additional benefit to the people who build them.

Government agencies, organizations, and everyday people are working together to help bats. As scientists continue to study bats, we will learn more ways to protect these incredible flying animals.

With our help, bats will continue to patrol the night skies for many years to come.

Words to Know

colonies (KAH-luh-neez) — large groups of animals that live together

deforestation (dee-for-iss-TAY-shuhn) — the removal or cutting down of forests

diverse (di-VURS) — having many different types or kinds

echolocation (eh-koh-loh-KAY-shuhn) — the process of using sound waves to locate surrounding objects

fossils (FOSS-uhlz) — the hardened remains of prehistoric plants and animals

fungus (FUHN-guhs) — a plantlike organism that has no leaves, flowers, roots, or chlorophyll, and grows on other plants or decaying matter

habitats (HAB-uh-tats) — the places where an animal or a plant is usually found

hibernating (HYE-bur-nay-ting) — sleeping through the winter in order to survive when temperatures are cold and food is hard to find

humidity (hyoo-MID-i-tee) — the amount of moisture in the air

insectivores (in-SEK-tuh-vorz) — animals that have insects as a regular part of their diet

mammals (MAM-uhlz) — warm-blooded animals that have hair or fur and usually give birth to live young

mating (MAYT-ing) — joining together to produce babies

megabats (MEG-uh-bats) — the suborder of bats that includes the large, plant-eating fruit bats and flying foxes

membranes (MEM-braynz) — very thin layers of tissue that line or cover certain organs or cells

microbats (MY-krow-bats) — the suborder of bats that includes smaller, meat-eating bats

migrate (MY-grayt) — to move from one area to another

nocturnal (nahk-TUR-nuhl) — active mainly at night

order (OR-duhr) — a category that groups different families of animals together according to similar traits that they share

parasites (PAR-uh-sites) — animals or plants that live on or inside of another animal or plant

predators (PREH-duh-turz) — animals that live by hunting other animals for food

prey (PRAY) — an animal that's hunted by another animal for food

primates (PRYE-mates) — any members of the group of mammals that includes monkeys, apes, and humans

pups (PUHPS) — baby bats

rabies (RAY-beez) — an often fatal disease that can affect humans, dogs, bats, and other warm-blooded animals

roosts (ROOSTS) — places where winged animals gather to rest at night

secluded (si-KLOO-did) — quiet and private, not seen or visited by many people

species (SPEE-sheez) — one of the groups into which animals and plants of the same genus are divided

superstitious (soo-pur-STISH-uhs) — describing a belief that explains the cause of something in a magical way that cannot be tested or proven

temperate (TEM-pur-it) — having a climate where the temperature is rarely very high or very low

torpor (TOR-pur) — a short-term decrease in activity that is similar to hibernation

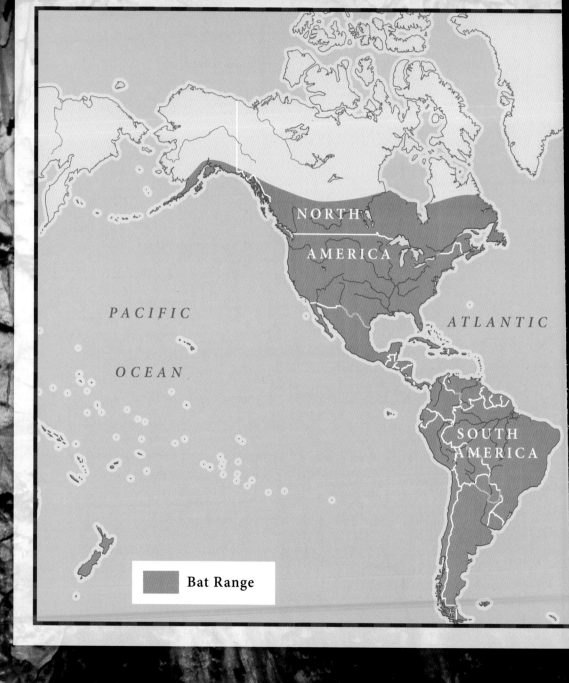

NORTH AMERICA

PACIFIC

OCEAN

ATLANTIC

SOUTH AMERICA

Bat Range

ARCTIC OCEAN

EUROPE

ASIA

AFRICA

PACIFIC OCEAN

OCEAN

INDIAN

OCEAN

AUSTRALIA

Find Out More

Books

Carson, Mary Kay. *The Bat Scientists*. Boston: Houghton Mifflin Books for Children, 2010.

Gish, Melissa. *Bats*. Mankato, MN: Creative Education, 2011.

Markovics, Joyce. *The Bat's Cave*. New York: Bearport Publishing, 2010.

Visit this Scholastic Web site for more information on bats:
www.factsfornow.scholastic.com
Enter the keyword **Bats**

Index

ancient bats, 30, *31*

babies. *See* pups.
bat boxes, 41
births, 26
blood, 9, 25
body temperatures, 18, 22
bumblebee bats, 9

caves, 6, 22, 38
Chiroptera order, 34
claws, 9
colonies, *20*, 21, 29, 41

deforestation, 37
diseases, *36*, 37, 38, *39*
disk-winged bats, 22

ears, 13, 34
echolocation, *12*, 13, 14, 34
eyes, 14, 26, 34

feet, 9, 22, 26
females, 21, 26, 29
flying, 6, *7*, 9, 10, *12*, 17, *24*, 26, 29,
     30, 37, *40*
flying foxes, 9, *9*, 17, 22, *32*, 33
food. *See* insects; milk; plants; prey.
fossils, 30, *31*
fruit bats, 14, 17, 25, 33, 34
fur, 6, *8*, 9, 26, *27*, 30

habitats, 6, 10, 14, 17, 18, 21, 22, 37
hairless bats, 9
harems, 21
hibernation, 18, *19*, 21, 38
humans, 6, 13, 30, 33, 37, 41
humidity, 22
hunting, 6, *7*, 13, 18, *24*, 29, 37, 38

insectivores, 25, 33, 34
insects, *7*, 9, *24*, 25, 29, 41

Kitti's hog-nosed bats, *9*

life spans, 10
long-eared bats, 18

males, 21
mating, 21
megabats, 34
Mexican free-tailed bats, 17
microbats, 34, *35*
migration, 17, 41
milk, 29

nocturnal species, 9
noses, 13, 34, 38, *39*

parasites, 38
plants, 6, 9, 14, *15*, *16*, 17, 22, 25, 29
predators, 10, *11*, 26
prey, 13, 25, 29, 37

(Index continued)

pups, 10, 26, *27*, *28*, 29

roosts, 6, 10, 18, *20*, 22, *23*, 29, 37, 41

seclusion, 10
sizes, 9, *9*, 18, 25, 29, 34
species, 6, 9, 10, 13, 17, 18, 21, 22, 25, 34
suction cups, 22

tail membrane, 25, 26
thumbs, 9, 22, 26
tongues, 14, *15*
torpor, 18

vampire bats, 25, *36*, 37

weight, 9, 18, 25, 29
white nose syndrome (WNS), 38, *39*, 41
wings, *8*, 9, 22, 26, 30

About the Author

Jennifer Zeiger lives in Chicago, Illinois, where she writes and edits books for children. She has always been fascinated by bats and the amazing things they can do.